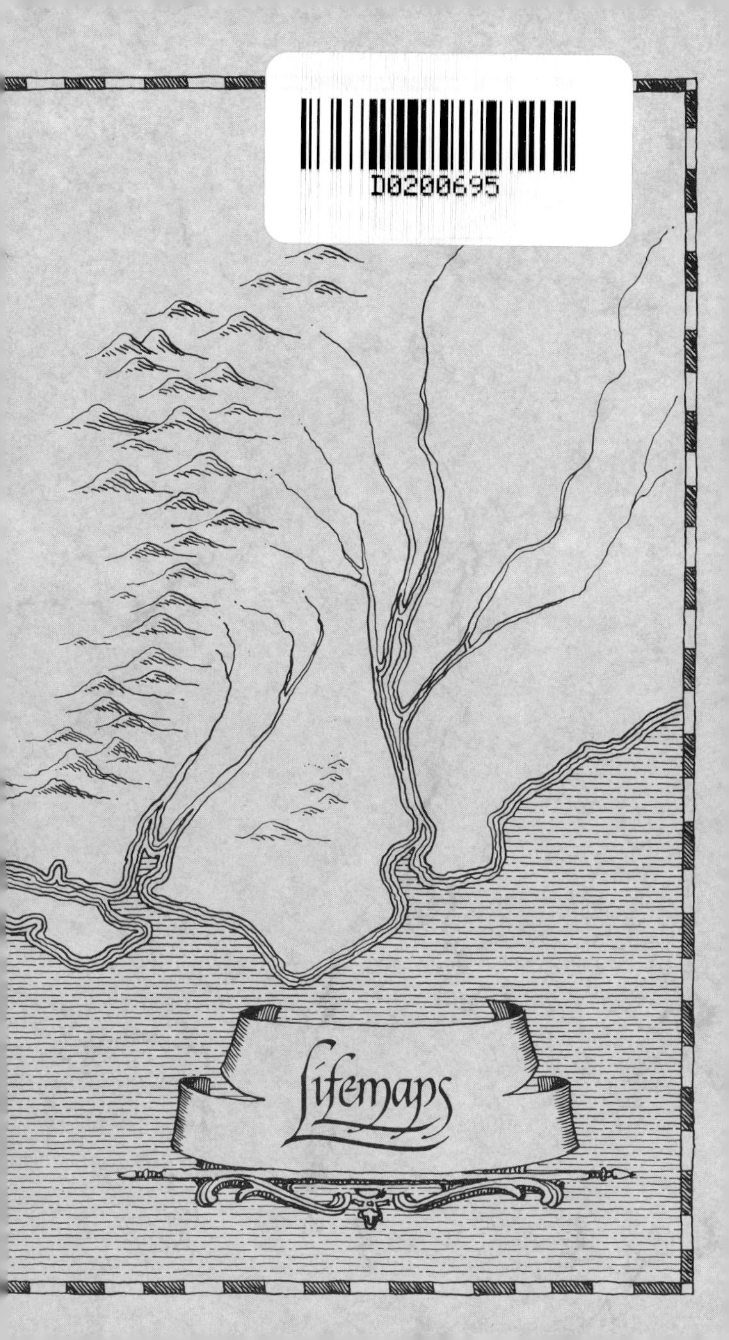
Lifemaps

Victory

Victory

A Winning Game Plan for Life

Chuck Swindoll

Lifemaps

WORD BOOKS
PUBLISHER
WACO, TEXAS
A DIVISION OF
WORD, INCORPORATED

VICTORY: A WINNING GAME PLAN FOR LIFE

Library of Congress Cataloging in Publication Data

Swindoll, Charles R.
Victory: a winning game plan for life.

(Lifemaps)
1. Christian life—1960– . 2. Success. I. Title.
BV4501.2.S897 1984 248.4 84–15329
ISBN 0–8499–0442–0

Printed in the United States of America

Surely you know that many runners take part in a race, but only one of them wins the prize. Run, then, in such a way as to win the prize. Every athlete in training submits to strict discipline, in order to be crowned with a wreath that will not last; but we do it for one that will last forever. That is why I run straight for the finish line; that is why I am like a boxer who does not waste his punches. I harden my body with blows and bring it under complete control, to keep myself from being disqualified after having called others to the contest.

1 Corinthians 9:24–27, TEV

INTRODUCTION

"Go for the gold!" Those are common words every four years as another series of Olympic Games arrives. The talk of winning is in the air. A ground swell of national pride increases to a fever pitch as muscular athletes all around the world continue their rigorous training. Dreams they have had for a lifetime drive them on with fresh determination—hour after hour, day after day.

Within the mind of each competitor is a scene as vivid and real as life itself. It takes place on a platform built for three. In the background is a heavy drum roll, then the playing of the majestic national anthem as the flag is hoisted. Standing tall on the center of the tiered platform is the personification of ecstasy and pride—an athlete with a large, round medal hanging to the waist. It's gold. It represents maximum fulfillment, the ultimate in sports. In that epochal moment, all the world watches with enviable delight as that individual embodies what everyone respects—*victory!* If it's true that all the world loves a lover, you can be sure of this—a victor is even more admired.

There is something deep within all of us that longs to win . . . to come out on top . . . to achieve that dream . . . to accomplish a major objective. But have you noticed something about victory? It seems amazingly elusive . . . at times, almost out of reach . . . maybe even exclusive—reserved for an elite class of humanity. These thoughts not only apply in the physical realm of athletics (how few of us know even one person who ever competed in the

Olympics!), but also in the spiritual realm of day-to-day Christianity. Strangely, the victorious Christian is both rare and remarkable.

It is precisely *that* realization that prompted me to write this book. My hope is that something I say in these pages will be the spark you've been needing to ignite the championship raw material within you. Those qualities have been dormant long enough. Personally, I am convinced that we Christians have within us sufficient power to handle and, when necessary, to overcome the odds. Rather than expecting us simply to cope, to grin and bear it, to grind our way along at a snail's pace, the Lord our God designed us to be victors, not victims, . . . to "overwhelmingly conquer" by the strength of His might.

If you're ready to believe that—and allow it to make a difference in your life—then you need to continue reading this book. As you proceed, keep the words of the psalm uppermost in your mind: "Through God we shall do valiantly . . ." (Ps. 60:12). I suppose if the psalmist had written it today, he would have said, "Through God, let's go for the gold!"

Chuck Swindoll
Fullerton, California

Victory

A Winning Game Plan for Life

"With God on our side, we will win"

Psalm 60:12, TEV

Christian books on victory are not uncommon. If you have browsed in a local bookstore recently you may have made that same observation. But if you took the time to read, in depth, the material each publication presented, there's a possibility you'd be more confused than helped. If it weren't so tragic, I'd find it rather humorous that many books on victory leave readers even more defeated and bewildered than they were to start with.

Some writers tell you to tighten up, others say loosen up. A few promote passivity, promising you power if you'll only "let go." But then there are those who say you need to "take up" special armor or "put off" the flesh or hold on longer or try harder or pray through. Invariably, there are always a few who chide you for not living above this world . . . yet, with equal vigor, some hold out the hope that you can have financial abundance ("God wants you to be rich!") if only you will avail yourself of some special blessings formula.

Is it any wonder that real victory seems elusive? Confusion and conquering cannot coexist.

As I begin this book I feel the need to clear the air of as much erroneous smog as possible. To do that, let's read some of the greatest verses in all the New Testament. Take your time. Let each verse soak in.

"O death, where is your victory? O death, where is your sting?" The sting of death is sin, and the power of sin is the law; but thanks be to God, who gives us the victory through our Lord Jesus Christ. Therefore, my beloved brethren, be steadfast, immovable, always abounding in the work of the Lord, knowing that your toil is not in vain in the Lord.

1 Corinthians 15:55–58

But thanks be to God, who always leads us in His triumph in Christ, and manifests through us the sweet aroma of the knowledge of Him in every place.

2 Corinthians 2:14

Finally, be strong in the Lord, and in the strength of His might. Put on the full armor of God, that you may be able to stand firm against the schemes of the devil. For our struggle is not against flesh and blood, but against the rulers, against the powers, against the world forces of this darkness, against the spiritual forces of wickedness in the heavenly places. Therefore, take up the full armor of God, that you may be able to resist in the evil day, and having done everything, to stand firm.

Ephesians 6:10–13

You are from God, little children, and have overcome them; because greater is He who is in you than he who is in the world.

1 John 4:4

What then shall we say to these things? If God is for us, who is against us? He who did not spare His own Son, but delivered Him up for us all, how will He not also with Him freely give us all things? Who will bring a charge against God's elect? God is the one who justifies; who is the one who condemns? Christ Jesus is He who died, yes, rather who was raised, who is at the right hand of God, who also intercedes for us. Who shall separate us from the love of Christ? Shall tribulation, or distress, or persecution, or famine, or nakedness, or peril, or sword? Just as it is written, "For Thy sake we are being put to death all day long; we were considered as sheep to be slaughtered." But in all these things we overwhelmingly conquer through Him who loved us.

Romans 8:31–37

FIVE THINGS VICTORY IS NOT

What great scriptures! Again and again we find references to victory in the New Testament. Of special interest to me is the section you just read from the letter to the Romans. Look closely. It is comprised of one question after another.

Each question calls forth a bold, confident answer. I cannot read those seven verses from Romans 8 without smiling. Without fail, they lift my spirit. What assurance! And did you notice that climactic ending? "We overwhelmingly conquer." Talk about winning!

But wait. The context doesn't sound very victorious. There are no triumphant soldiers with fixed bayonets or smoking cannons. Look again at what's pictured there, and try not to be surprised. It's *sheep*—sheep ready to be slaughtered!

And a closer look reveals that the battlefield is not what you'd call filled with the spoils of victory. There is tribulation. There is affliction. There is pain, and hardship, and hunger, along with a lack of sufficient clothing; and there is even death.

Rather than an impressive display of power—the kind of power we usually associate with success and victory—there is consistent inner strength, incredible determination, quiet confidence, solid security, and unswerving love. It is in and through *these* things that "we overwhelmingly conquer."

All this prompts me to list several of the things victory is not.

1. *Victory is not a once-for-all, automatic inheritance.* Christians need the reminder that the life God provides—commonly called the "abundant life"—is not one continuous, unbroken chain of victorious experiences. It is available, but it is not automatic. The strength we need to handle life's pressures is there to be

claimed, but in no way should we think of the Christian way of life as "instant success."

2. *Victory is not an emotional "high."* You'll look in vain to find a lot of feelings in the Romans 8 section of Scripture. On the contrary, you'll find statements of assurance, strong affirmation, and confidence-building facts. For the Christian, victory doesn't rely on being psyched up or in the mood.

3. *Victory is not a dream reserved for super-saints.* You'll find no hint of class distinction or partiality here. All that's needed to qualify is being a sheep.

4. *Victory is not an independent achievement.* Pay close attention to this. Unlike the lonely runner on the track, the Christian who conquers does so "through Him who loved us." Or, as we read elsewhere, "Thanks be to God, who gives us the victory through our Lord Jesus Christ" (1 Cor. 15:57).

5. *Victory is not something that happens to us while we passively wait.*

I cannot think of a more subtle adversary of victory than passivity. To make matters worse, there are many who peddle a nice-sounding message of passivity; and rather than being refused, they are being warmly embraced by many unsuspecting souls. An old axiom remains as true as the day it was first stated, "To the victor belong the responsibilities."

We may be sheep and we may find it altogether essential to draw upon our Lord for the persistence and the power we need, but, I repeat, *none of that is automatic.* Passivity is an enemy to anyone who hopes to live a life of victory. It's as foolish for the believer to think that conquering will "just happen" as it would be to imagine an Olympic champion standing on the center of the winner's platform and saying, "I really had nothing to do with this gold medal. Just a few minutes ago I looked down and there it was, hanging around my neck." What a joke! The victorious

Christian, like the victorious athlete, wins because he or she is deliberately and personally involved—from start to finish—in a process that leads to victory.

Make no mistake about it, victory is not automatic.

Enough of the negatives. Let's spend the balance of our time thinking about the positives—the specifics involved in a life marked by victory. To begin with, I can think of no better scripture to consider than the ninth chapter of 1 Corinthians, actually the final four verses of that chapter.

Do you not know that those who run in a race all run, but only one receives the prize? Run in such a way that you may win. And everyone who competes in the games exercises self-control in all things. They then do it to receive a perishable wreath, but we an imperishable. Therefore I run in such a way, as not without aim; I box in such a way, as not beating the air; but I buffet my body and make it my slave, lest possibly, after I have preached to others, I myself should be disqualified.

1 Corinthians 9:24–27

FOUR THINGS VICTORY INCLUDES

Rather than plunging into these verses in 1 Corinthians 9, let's spend a few minutes getting our bearings. This chapter begins with Paul's declaring that as an apostle he has certain rights and privileges. As is true with high-ranking officers in the military, apostleship carried with it a lot of clout. He not only had those rights, he was free to exercise them to their fullest.

> Am I not free? Am I not an apostle? Have I not seen Jesus our Lord? Are you not my work in the Lord? If to others I am not an apostle, at least I am to you; for you are the seal of my apostleship in the Lord. My defense to those who examine me is this: Do we not have the right to eat and drink? Do we not have the right to take along a believing wife, even as

> the rest of the apostles, and the brothers of the Lord, and Cephas? Or do only Barnabas and I not have the right to refrain from working? (1 Cor. 9:1–6).

That's clear enough. As an apostle those rights were his to claim. Yet . . .

> If others share the right over you, do we not more? Nevertheless, we did not use this right . . . (v. 12).

Although the man had rights and privileges, he purposely chose not to take them. He refused to take full advantage of them. Why? Well, that's the subject of the remainder of this book. Basically, there are two reasons. The first was a public one; the second, private. One was for the sake of others. The other was for his own sake.

> If others share the right over you, do we not more? Nevertheless, we did not use this right, but we endure all things, that we may cause no hindrance to the gospel of Christ (v. 12).

The first reason why Paul resisted his rights and limited himself was *for the sake of winning more people to Christ.* Remember his comments regarding this?

> For though I am free from all men, I have made myself a slave to all, that I might win the more. And to the Jews I became as a Jew, that I might win Jews; to those who are under the Law, as under the Law, though not being myself under the Law, that I might win those who are under the Law; to those who are without law, as without law, though not being without the law of God but under the law of Christ, that I might win those who are without law. To the weak I became weak, that I might win the weak; I have become all things to all men, that I may by all means

> save some. And I do all things for the sake of the gospel, that I may become a fellow-partaker of it (1 Cor. 9:19–23).

His first reason for applying such self-control is amplified in these five verses. He desired to win the maximum number of people to Christ. I hope you noticed the frequently repeated phrase, "That I might win . . . that I might win." But it is Paul's second reason for choosing not to take full advantage of his rights that ties in so perfectly with the subject of this book: He limited his liberty *for the sake of winning personal victory.* His life of self-control was motivated by a desire to "overwhelmingly conquer" as a man . . . as a child of God. Let's probe this thought by examining these final verses very carefully. Please read them again, this time using the *Amplified Bible.*

> Do you not know that in a race all the runners compete, but [only] one receives

> the prize? So run [your race] that you may lay hold [of the prize] and make it yours. Now every athlete who goes into training conducts himself temperately and restricts himself in all things. They do it to win a wreath that will soon wither, but we [do it to receive a crown of eternal blessedness] that cannot wither. Therefore I do not run uncertainly—without definite aim. I do not box as one beating the air and striking without an adversary. But [like a boxer] I buffet my body—handle it roughly, discipline it by hardships—and subdue it, for fear that after proclaiming to others the Gospel and things pertaining to it, I myself should become unfit—not stand the test and be unapproved—and rejected [as a counterfeit] (1 Cor. 9:24–27).

I have thought about those words for years. And I can hardly remember hearing anyone ever speak on them with much enthusiasm. Yet, the more I meditate on these verses, the more significant they become. It's almost as if the great Apostle Paul is giving us his credo in a few words. This, in my opinion, is a condensed version of how the man was able to stay on track in spite of circumstances that would have buckled the knees of most. What a spiritual champion!

I find here at least four essentials that comprise a life of victory—action, aim, discipline, reward. First, let's take a look at *action*.

Action

These four verses at the end of 1 Corinthians 9 drip with the sweat of an athlete. You can almost hear the grunts and feel the perspiration—those agonizing sounds of the track, the court, the ring. There is enthusiasm woven throughout the fabric of these words. Picture the scenes of activity as you read:

Verse 24: ". . . those who run in a
race. . . .
Run . . . that you may win."

Verse 25: ". . . Everyone who
competes in the games
excercises self-control in all
things."

Verse 26: ". . . I run . . . I box. . . ."

Verse 27: ". . . I buffet my body and
make it my slave. . . ."

Maybe you are as intrigued as I was with the mention of "the games" in verse 25. My interest was heightened by the use of a particular Greek term translated "competes" in the same verse. The term is *agonizomai,* the very word from which we get our English words "agony" and "agonize." Whatever "the games" has reference to, the whole idea of "agonizing competition" is attached to it.

In my research I discovered some fascinating information that makes all this vibrate with color and life. I found, for example, that athletic contests were common in the Greek world. Not only did the Greeks have their *Olympics*, but every three years they flocked into the stadiums in ancient Corinth to witness the *Isthmian* games as well. As is true today, all the athletes in those ancient games underwent a strict training program for many, many months.

The games consisted of numerous athletic contests, including running—both short dashes and lengthy marathons—and an event called "leaping"—much like our long jump, no doubt. In addition, the games featured spear throwing (answering, perhaps, to the javelin today), wrestling, boxing, chariot racing, and even racing in armor, plus other competitive contests.

I found that in order to qualify for the games of ancient Greece, athletes were obligated to take an oath. This oath stated that they had trained for at least ten months. They also swore they would not resort to any deceitful or unfair "tricks" in the contests they entered. As is true today, those athletes watched their diets with great care, and the regimen of their workouts was nothing short of excruciating. With earnestness of purpose and self-sacrificial resolve, they trained for those games. To the sports-minded Greek, the gymnasium was the center of interest, so much so, in fact, that his life was saturated with the spirit of competition. The action-oriented society of the ancient Greek world was more like our active, fitness-crazed American lifestyle than most of us would ever believe.[1] And it's within that set of word pictures that Paul writes of victory.

Again, at the risk of too much repetition, I remind you that a life characterized by overwhelming victory is not a laid-back life. It is rather an active (dare I say *aggressive?*) pursuit. This brings us to the next essential in a life of victory—*aim*.

Aim

Read a few more statements and phrases from 1 Corinthians 9:

Verse 24: ". . . All run, but only one receives the prize.
Run in such a way that you may win."

Verse 26: ". . . I run in such a way, as not without aim; I box in such a way, as not beating the air."

Clearly, the runner is obliged to stay on course if winning is in view. The eye is intent on the final tape at the end. Those who run, run toward it—they aim at it. The same is true of the boxer. If we were to put verse 26 in today's terms, we'd say, "I box, but I don't shadowbox!" As one authority describes it, ". . . 'No air-smiter': he uses his fists as one in deadly earnest, and does not miss: he plants his blow." [2]

Paul's point is clear. The Christian faces a host of very real enemies. Few people have pictured them more clearly than John Bunyan in *The Pilgrim's Progress.* With relentless regularity each foe came upon Christian and brought along its own subtle snare. In order for him to make it to the Celestial City, he had to keep his aim clear. Losing sight of the goal and mere "shadowboxing" would only weaken his walk. So it is with us in the evil days of the twentieth century.

Someone once said, "So far from the world being a goddess in petticoats, it is rather a devil in a strait waistcoat." It's true—the world we live in is downright devilish, full of potholes, traps, and subtle snares designed to get the Christian off course. Long enough have we courted its fancy and smiled back into its alluring face! The believer who makes it his or her determined aim to love God and to live victoriously for Christ will be forced to get tough and decide, if necessary, to stand alone.

Isaac Watts put it this way:

> Am I a soldier of the cross,
> A follower of the Lamb?
> And shall I fear to own His cause,
> Or blush to speak His name?
>
> Are there no foes for me to face?
> Must I not stem the flood?
> Is this vile world a friend to grace,
> To help me on to God?

Good questions—tough-minded, sinewy questions. Those who choose to walk in victory must answer them almost daily—sometimes hourly.

Personally, it helps me to set goals. To achieve anything significant in my life, I find I must first determine a set of objectives. Each objective, as it is reached, moves me systematically closer to the ultimate goal. This goal-setting philosophy or mindset is what I mean by *aim.*

Victory requires it. Victory isn't discovered, it's achieved. Winning a battle is never something troops stumble upon; it's the result of a strategy, a carefully thought-through plan of attack. The same analogy holds true for a ball game. It's called a "game plan." High-priced, brilliant, seasoned coaches spend hours every week thinking about and then communicating the plan. As the players enter the contest, they have literally *memorized* the plan. To use Paul's words, they "run in such a way, as not without aim."

May I be so bold as to ask, "Where are you going?" and "How do you plan to get there?" Even more specifically,

"What is your strategy for handling the temptations you are sure to face?" I am convinced that these and other related questions must be asked and answered if we hope to be among the ranks of those who "overwhelmingly conquer."

Sound too tight? Too rigid? You're wondering if even Paul lived with such a well-thought-through game plan? I find that question answered when I read the words he wrote from a dungeon shortly before he was beheaded.

> . . . I am already being poured out as a drink offering, and the time of my departure has come. I have fought the good fight, I have finished the course, I have kept the faith (2 Tim. 4:6–7).

Aim and victory walk in step with each other. But equally important for a life of victory is discipline.

Discipline

Discipline is a term that is nothing more than a "dirty word" for self-control. It's one of several hated terms of our times. But have you noticed how often it comes up in the testimonies of those who win?

The great apostle says that he willingly forfeited his apostolic rights for the sake of winning more (1 Cor. 9:19–23). That took discipline. In 2 Timothy 2:10, he mentions that he endured all things in order to reach his objective. That certainly took discipline. As we read earlier in 1 Corinthians 9:25, Paul says that those who compete in the games exercise "self-control in all things." Again, discipline is the key.

- No runner completes the training or a race without it.
- No weight-loss program is maintained without it.

- No human body is kept fit without it.
- No mind is sharpened without it.
- No temptation is overcome without it.

So who are we kidding? Without discipline, we can kiss victory good-by. And the alternative to discipline is dangerously close to an irresponsible lifestyle (hardly the model expected of the authentic Christian). This was brought home to me rather forcefully when I read a statement that originally appeared in the *Wheaton College Bulletin:*

> The undisciplined is a headache to himself and a heartache to others, and is unprepared to face the stern realities of life.

If you are ready to put a stop to mediocrity, to replace excuses with fresh determination . . . procrastination with tough-minded perseverance, I can assure you that victory will become an attainable reality rather than a distant dream. Disciplined persistence is a major factor if you hope to be a winner.

The late Ray Kroc, founder of the world-famous McDonald's hamburger chain, loved the same statement that football coach Vince Lombardi often quoted.

> Press on: Nothing in the world can take the place of persistence. Talent will not; nothing is more common than unsuccessful individuals with talent. Genius will not; unrewarded genius is almost a proverb. Education will not; the world is full of educated derelicts. Persistence and determination alone are omnipotent.[3]

And before you are tempted to think, "I'm too old to start now," I should remind you that Kroc didn't start

McDonald's until he was fifty-two. And lest you think a late start offers few benefits, he reached the billion-dollar mark in just twenty-two years. By the way, it took IBM forty-six years to reach its first billion in revenue, and it took Xerox sixty-two years. So starting late could have its advantages!

But wait. We're not talking about making money, we're talking about building a life. The subject is victory—personal victory, becoming an individual who develops a will to win, who draws upon the inestimable power of the living God to face life head-on, regardless.

One of the many exciting aspects of my life as the pastor of a church is to witness the spiritual growth of various people. Sometimes those who grow the fastest and become the best models of strength and determination are those whose circumstances are extremely difficult.

One such individual comes to my mind. She is a single parent, the product of an abusive home and intense marital conflicts. Emotionally starved, this young woman stumbled into our fellowship several years ago and found encouragement, support, and hope. Christ became her Savior and her never-failing friend. She went through long months of professional counseling with a dedicated Christian therapist. With an incredible will to go on, she began to drink in the Scriptures. She opened her arms to others in need. She became an authentic, flesh-and-blood example of remarkable change—the kind of changes only God could make. In place of moral compromise, she now lives in purity. Instead of insecurity and low self-esteem, she believes in herself . . . she sees worth and value in her life. She has become victorious! Her latest achievement: a twenty-pound weight loss during the hot summer months that just passed.

In a letter of gratitude that she recently wrote to me, she mentioned the importance of discipline, or persistence, as she called it:

> Without persistence I would be dead. I would have given in to the despair of hopelessness that was my life. I would have surely died from loneliness. . . . Victory is the result.

Then she added:

> This has been another incredibly challenging year as a mother of two teenagers, as a single parent, as a student of psychology at CSFU. I graduate next May and then want to go on to get my masters and MFCC license. Talk about persistence! If I hadn't had it, I'd have buckled under a long time ago.

Isn't that magnificent! If only you could have known this lady several years ago. But now, with determination, she is off and running.

Is such a goal worth it? I mean, in the final analysis, does this kind of tough-minded victory pay off? The answer is clear when we look at the crowning point of all—*reward,* the fourth essential in a life of victory.

Reward

Let me remind you of something Paul mentions regarding reward:

> They then do it to receive a perishable wreath, but we an imperishable (1 Cor. 9:25).

I'm not sure that so few words ever had greater meaning. The contrast is nothing short of phenomenal. The "they" refers to those athletes who strain, sweat, train, and finally win. Their reward? A perishable wreath that withers and is soon forgotten.

Oh, there were a few other perks I should mention. A herald proclaimed the victor's name as well as his home. The winner was awarded five hundred *drachmae* from Athens, a triumphal entrance into his hometown, and a perpetual seat of honor at all succeeding games. Tradition tells us that his children were educated free of charge, and he was relieved of taxation and military duty for the rest of his life . . . not to mention the fame that was sure to follow the victor all his days.[4]

But all of that would eventually perish. It had no lasting value, no eternal dimension. It's still true today. There is no trophy that will not ultimately settle into dust. The jeweled boxer's belt is worn only temporarily—until another world champion is crowned. There is no Super Bowl ring that will resist tarnishing . . . no honor, no matter how impressive, that will benefit anyone beyond the grave. All the applause, all the ink from sportswriters' pens, all the talk from small cafes to swanky, sophisticated clubs will finally fade. The best that can be said for it is that it's "a perishable wreath."

Not so for the Christian conqueror! Our victory wreath is designated by God as "imperishable." It will come in the form of a crown called a "crown of righteousness." Read these words slowly, preferably aloud:

> I have fought the good fight, I have finished the course, I have kept the faith; in the future there is laid up for me the crown of righteousness, which the Lord, the righteous Judge, will award to me on that day; and not only to me, but also to all who have loved His appearing (2 Tim. 4:7–8).

What a promise!

And if I read God's plan for our future correctly, I note that those saints "crowned" for walking in victory will, one day in glory,

> . . . fall down before Him who sits on the throne, and will worship Him who lives forever and ever, and will cast their crowns before the throne, saying, "Worthy art Thou, our Lord and our God, to receive glory and honor and power; for Thou didst create all things, and because of Thy will they existed, and were created" (Rev. 4:10–11).

There are times in my life when I close my eyes and try to imagine such a scene. When I do, I often recall the words of a grand old hymn of the church which is seldom sung these days—"The Sands of Time" by Anne R. Cousin.

> The sands of time are sinking,
> The dawn of heaven breaks;
> The summer morn I've sighed for,
> The fair, sweet morn awakes;

Dark, dark hath been the midnight,
But dayspring is at hand,
And glory, glory dwelleth
In Immanuel's land.

The Bride eyes not her garment,
But her dear Bridegroom's face;
I will not gaze at glory
But on my King of grace.
Not at the crown He giveth
But on His pierced hand,
The Lamb is all the glory
Of Immanuel's land.

If all we had to keep us going were the sweat and grind of a hot track or the demanding hours and sacrificial diet of a relentless training schedule, it's doubtful any of us could make it. Victory would, indeed, be only a dream for supermen and wonder-women. But God promises His people a reward that will never perish.

Who wouldn't want such a reward? Compared to God's eternal benefits, who would ever opt for the temporary? But how? How is it possible for mere human beings to connect with such eternal values? What's necessary for a life of victory?

THOU ART MY VICTORY

I prayed for help, I prayed for strength,
I prayed for victory:
I prayed for patience and for love,
For true humility
But as I prayed, my dying Christ
By faith I seemed to see,
And as I gazed my glad heart cried,
"All things are mine, thro' Thee!"

If He doth dwell within my heart,
Why need I strength implore?
The Giver of all grace is mine,
And shall I ask for more?
And need I pray for victory,
When He who conquered death
Dwells in my very inmost soul,
Nearer indeed than breath?

Oh help me, Lord, to realize
That Thou art all in all;
That I am more than conqueror
In great things and in small
No need have I but Thou hast met
Upon the cruel tree.
Oh precious, dying, risen Lord,
Thou art my victory!

—Avis B. Christiansen

THREE THINGS THAT EQUIP US FOR VICTORY

According to Scripture three things are needed for a life of victory:

- Birth
- Faith
- Truth

> For whatever is born of God overcomes the world; and this is the victory that has overcome the world—our faith. And who is the one who overcomes the world, but he who believes that Jesus is the Son of God? . . . And it is the Spirit who bears witness, because the Spirit is the truth (1 John 5:4–5, 7).

In order to enter into the ranks of the victorious, we must be "born of God." Jesus called this process being "born anew" and/or being "born again." This occurs when I accept the gift of eternal life made possible by Jesus' death and resurrection . . . when I, personally, ask the Son of God to become my Savior from sin. Birth must precede everything. With it I receive Christ's life, power, and cleansing.

Then comes faith. I draw upon the power that is in me. I no longer operate on the basis of human strength, but by faith, I convert to divine power. And the difference in the two is like that between rumbling along in a twenty-five-ton tank and lifting off the runway in a Phantom jet. Look again at what was said in 1 John 5:4.

> . . . and this is the victory that has overcome the world—our faith.

It is all made possible by the truth . . . believing the truth; living in the truth;

allowing the truth to invade, reshape, and cultivate our lives anew.

Tell me, have you had such a birth?

Well then, if so, are you operating on faith?

And the truth—is it the truth you are claiming?

It's time for action. Quit hiding behind those excuses! Stop telling yourself it's too late. It is never too late to start doing what is right. Start now. The alternative is too grim to consider. Trust me, you can move from the realm of defeat and discouragement to victory and hope if you will simply take action now. Aim high. Go hard after God!

MAKE ME THY FUEL

From prayer that asks that I may be
Sheltered from winds that beat on Thee,
From fearing when I should aspire,
From faultering when I should climb higher,
From silken self, O Captain, free
Thy soldier who would follow Thee.

From subtle love of softening things,
From easy choices, weakenings,
Not thus are spirits fortified,
Not this way went the Crucified,
From all that dims Thy Calvary,
O Lamb of God, deliver me.

Give me the love that leads the way,
The faith that nothing can dismay,
The hope no disappointments tire,
The passion that will burn like fire,
Let me not sink to be a clod:
Make me Thy fuel, Flame of God.

—Amy Carmichael

A CONCLUDING STORY

Wilma was born prematurely. This produced complications that resulted in her contracting double pneumonia (twice) and scarlet fever. But the worst was a bout with polio which left her with a crooked left leg and a foot twisted inward. Metal leg braces; stares from neighborhood kids; and six years of bus rides to Nashville for treatments could have driven this young girl into a self-made shell. But she refused.

Wilma kept dreaming. And she was determined not to allow her disability to get in the way of her dreams. Maybe her determination was generated by the faith of her Christian mother who often said "Honey, the most important thing in life is for you to believe it and keep on trying."

By age eleven, Wilma decided to "believe it." And through sheer determination and an indomitable spirit to persevere, *regardless,* she forced herself to learn how to walk without the braces.

At age twelve she made a wonderful discovery: Girls could run and jump and play ball just like boys! Her older sister Yvonne was quite good at basketball, so Wilma decided to challenge her on the court. She began to improve. The two of them ultimately went out for the same school team. Yvonne made the final twelve, but Wilma didn't. However, because her father wouldn't allow Yvonne to travel with the team without her sister as a "chaperone," Wilma found herself often in the presence of the coach.

One day she built up enough nerve to confront the man with her magnificent obsession—her lifetime dream. She blurted out, "If you will give me ten minutes of your time every day—and only ten minutes—I'll give you a world-class athlete."

He took her up on the offer. The result is history. Young Wilma finally won a starting position on the basketball squad; and when that season ended, she decided to try out for the track team. What a decision!

In her first race, she beat her girl friend. Then she beat all the girls in her high school . . . then, *every* high school girl in the state of Tennessee. Wilma was only fourteen, but already a champion.

Shortly thereafter, although still in high school, she was invited to join the Tigerbelle's track team at Tennessee State University. She began a serious training program after school and on weekends. As she improved, she continued winning short dashes and the 440-yard relay.

Two years later she was invited to try out for the Olympics. She qualified and ran in the 1956 games at Melbourne, Australia. She won a bronze medal as her team placed third in the 400-meter relay. It was a bittersweet victory. She had won—but she decided that next time she would "go for the gold."

I could skip four years and hurry on to Rome, but that would not do justice to the whole story. Wilma realized that victory would require an enormous amount of commitment, sacrifice, and discipline. To give her "the winner's edge" as a world-class athlete, she began a do-it-yourself program similar to the one she had employed to get herself out of those leg braces. Not only did she run at six and ten every morning and three every afternoon, she would often sneak down the dormitory fire escape from eight to ten o'clock and run on the track before bedtime. Week after week, month in and month out, Wilma maintained the same grueling schedule . . . for over twelve hundred days.

Now we're ready for Rome. When the sleek, trim, young black lady, only twenty years old, walked out onto the field, she was ready. She had paid the price. Even those eighty thousand fans could sense the spirit of victory. It was electrifying. As she began her warm-up sprints, a cadenced chant began to emerge from the stands: "Vilma . . . Vilma . . . VILMA!" They were as confident as she that she would win.

And win she did! She breezed to an easy victory in the 100-meter dash. Then she won the 200-meter dash. And finally, she anchored the U.S. women's team to another first-place finish in the 400-meter relay. Three gold medals—she was the first woman in history ever to win three gold medals in track-and-field. I should add that each of the three races was won in world-record time.[5]

The little crippled girl from Clarksville, Tennessee, was now a world-class athlete. Wilma Rudolph had decided she wouldn't allow her disability to disqualify her; instead, she chose to pay the price for victory and "go for the gold."

Christ offers us a winning game plan for life. It is not a distant dream, but a present reality. As He comes into our lives, He brings all the power we will ever need, all the confidence, all the hope, all the determination, everything. He, the Ultimate Victor, smiles with affirmation and applauds our every decision to draw upon His all-sufficiency.

If Wilma Rudolph could muster the courage to shed those leg braces and overcome one hurdle after another in her world-class pursuit of the gold, I am convinced we can too. And the kind of gold God promises us will never tarnish, never diminish in significance, never fade away.

If you are ready, I'll run with you. Let's start today.

NOTES

1. See Frank Ely Gaebelein, *The Expositor's Bible Commentary* (Grand Rapids, MI: The Zondervan Corporation, 1976), p. 246; John S. Howson, *The Metaphors of St. Paul* (London, England: Strahan & Co., Publishers, 1869), pp. 125–176; The Rev. Leon Morris, *The First Epistle of Paul to the Corinthians* (Grand Rapids, MI: Wm. B. Eerdmans Publishing Company, 1978), pp. 136–140; Victor C. Pfitzner, *Paul and the Agon Motif* (Leiden, Netherlands: E. J. Brill, 1967), pp. 134–156; and Merrill F. Unger, *Unger's Bible Dictionary* (Chicago: Moody Press, 1957), p. 389.

2. Archibald Robertson and Alfred Plummer, *A Critical and Exegetical Commentary on the First Epistle of St. Paul to the Corinthians,* The International Critical Commentary (Edinburgh, England: T. & T. Clark, 1914), p. 196.

3. Ray A. Kroc, *Grinding It Out* (New York: Berkley, 1978), p. 201.

4. Merrill F. Unger, *Unger's Bible Dictionary* (Chicago: Moody Press, 1957), p. 389.

5. Wilma Rudolph, *Wilma: The Story of Wilma Rudolph,* ed. Bud Greenspan (New York: New American Library, Inc., 1977).

ABOUT THE AUTHOR

Ordained into the gospel ministry in 1963, Dr. Charles R. Swindoll has developed a popular expository pulpit style characterized by a clear and accurate presentation of Scripture, with a marked emphasis on the practical application of the Bible to everyday living, making God's truths a reality in the lives of hurting people.

Raised in Houston, Texas, and having originally pursued a career in engineering, Dr. Swindoll entered Dallas Theological Seminary in 1959 and graduated four years later with honors. In June 1977 an honorary doctor of divinity degree was conferred on him by Talbot Theological Seminary in La Mirada, California.

Since 1971 Dr. Swindoll has been senior pastor at the First Evangelical Free Church of Fullerton, California.

Currently, Dr. Swindoll's ministry is shared internationally through an extensive cassette tape distribution and a thirty-minute daily radio broadcast—"Insight for Living"—now being aired more than seven hundred times each day worldwide. "Insight for Living" received the prestigious Award of Merit from National

Religious Broadcasters for the outstanding religious broadcast in 1982.

A growing list of Dr. Swindoll's published works include the Christian film, *People of Refuge;* a six-message film series, *Strengthening Your Grip;* and more than fourteen books, among which are *Dropping Your Guard; Strengthening Your Grip; Improving Your Serve; Strike the Original Match;* and *Three Steps Forward, Two Steps Back.* Also available are sixteen booklets: *Anger, Attitudes, Commitment, Demonism, Destiny, Divorce, Eternal Security, God's Will, Hope, Integrity, Leisure, Sensuality, Singleness, Stress, Tongues,* and *Woman.*

Dr. Swindoll and his wife, Cynthia, have four children—Curtis and Charissa (both married) and Colleen and Chuck (both students still living at home). The Swindolls reside in Fullerton, California.

N